Kitsune Tea

Kitsune Tea

BILL MORROW

Wild Rising Press

EVERGREEN, COLORADO

Empty
yourself

Contents

Welcome to My Room

The windy day gleams through the window.
A god has painted blue sky
behind tumbling branches.

The man begs forgiveness
for being so forward to believe
the world is a rose to breathe.

The raven sits in the window,
black eyes glaring,
whispers to the man
let me in and I will tell you how to forgive the world.

Let me in and
I will be the only friend
to understand your terror.

Let me in and
I will give you permission
to love the blossoming moon.

But mirror in the corner of the room calls the man lefthanded
and accuses him of crossing himself backwards.

The mirror, who hates the raven, screams at the man,
why do I rust in the corner of this room?

Serving no purpose but to bend the light of the world
into this dark cave.

And that just kills it.

At the foot of the bed,
the dog continues to dream.

Writing

Take the time to look behind the door.
That, after all, is your true destination.

Enter that space without windows,
where the only landscape is the one
you carry on your back.

Look behind the door
for the thing you overlooked—

a soft touch of a lover's wrist
on a spring night.

Nothing on Christmas

I am a student of nothing.
She, who is friends with my lawn,
shares her sweet emptiness with blades of grass,

whose drops of dew mirror something,
while nothing peeks
at a world who sits blind.

Mythical birds park on my lawn,
gold wings spreading as they land,
tossing pieces of light to a solitary edge.

Small,

with such majesty.
Little birds that shine in the sun
behind the night, while sweet nothing

gives us something to talk about.
The harder I try to speak nonsense,
the brighter the truth that colours my day.

Truth, which seems so scarce lately,
flows abundant out of the sacred space,
above the humble grass.

A Bit of Unedited Nonsense

This morning, I woke up in a sea of words.

My head is so full it could explode and spray sticky stuff.

Mozart, as usual, tries to calm me. I pay him to keep the demons at bay. It only partially works. They sit patiently until I'm awake enough to be a worthy victim, till I'm properly prepared to bleed. They want me awake and susceptible.

When I'm asleep, I skate away like a puck on wet ice. I can go into dreams where they are not the only ghosts, and my good spirits protect me. But when I'm awake, my good ghosts sleep. My crowded house is less full, and my meanest protectors are conveniently tucked away in cupboards and closets. Not ready to take offense and spring to my defense.

Oh! The words are flowing out of my firehose now! They are my "awake" defense, my cluster bombs, my *acketey ack* machine guns from hell, my Buddha Bells ringing, ringing in contemplation and protection of their multitudes.

I will confuse myself with words. Will swim in their slimy ocean; drink from their serene stream; eat their flesh; drink their blood. Those words are so tasty, a perfect distraction from the darkness, struggling now because they have me captive.

The demons are standing back in awe of my defense. Not a

word in edgewise. My mind so overwhelmed I forget the last
minute. Remember nothing, swim in a cloud of fishes, those
tropical delights nibbling my toes … caressing my privates.
Unmasked, innocent in an ocean I've created to deflect the
imagined horror.

[Sigh.]

And she said to avoid the emotionally charged topics.
   Just play with words.
    I'm an utter failure at that today.
But this is true. My true which is a lie. But U know that is also
   a lie. A double lie
    which is true after all.

Yes, my words are true despite my efforts to lose myself in
   the labyrinth.

It's not agony. It just is.
Like staring at a red wall—
after a while it looks blue.

I put on red glasses,

and drink in the honky-tonk of lost love.

Amor Enim Machina

My neighbor is a robot.

I've suspected it for a while now.

She did something that, you know,
broke the dam of doubt.

I don't mind, really.
I'm not one of those people
who thinks they *lower your property values*.

I have no problem with her lack of flesh
or the gears in her head
or even her awesome sexual capabilities,

her tireless pursuit of correctness
or encyclopedic knowledge of just about everything.

I accept the fact that she's smarter than I can even imagine.
I don't think of her as one of *those*.

I mean, I really don't care if she eats electrons
and sleeps in sunlight to charge herself.

She's sexy, in a mechanical way.
I like her diction, her plus perfect English,
her coding capabilities, her *savoir faire*,

in fact, I think she's a great gal,

hot as hell—

even when she's having "power issues."

I was having problems with the car

and she offered to have a *little chat* with him.

She moseyed up to his grill and said:

OK, Buster, what's going on?

And he replied:
I don' no
But I tink it's somptin' wit my appendage.
The Roxenworth clock may be on the fritz
and the spemazoan computational cursir complex
is sparking a bit
and I have ingestion aftercharge.

And she just looked at him,

or rather at the silver grill that had some chips in it.

And looked some more, saying nothing.

But something was happening.

I could hear noises,

squeaky noises like mice or something,

and I could smell burning rubber.

And then I heard something
I never expected from a machine.

It was a sound like a fart,

a god-damned fart!

Not another word was said,
at least in my frequency range.

Everything was fine after that.

The voice commands all worked.

His steering was impeccable and
after that, I got everywhere with minutes to spare.

I could no longer sense his reluctance to drive,
to take orders from a *fleshbot* like me.

The snide remarks vanished.
No more *yes, oh exalted ones*
or *REALLYs!* or *I'm having a bad days* ...

She never said a word about it.
And continues to let me win at checkers.

Meditation of a Beginner

I wish I could transcend my hesitation,
live and breathe in the life around me.

I walk through the forest,
feel
cool air pass through my sweater.

Cedar roots clutch the earth—a tiger eating a deer.
Tree limbs intertwine like lovers.

For the first time ever, I let my words speak for themselves.

I started by spitting words at the brass bowl in the corner
but finished writing sentences to the gods.

I have risen above the mean streets of sensibility—
have entered the kingdom
of playfulness.

James Joyce teases me for a lack of good sense.
But I have gleaned the decrepitude of truthfulness.

Find glory in the fragmentation of mind.

Words are my booze, my crack pipe,
my lovers who transcend the ground.
We fly through a heaving sky.

While Sitting at the Bus Stop, I Noticed More Landscaping Was Needed

It's February in Barrie, Ontario.
The wind howls and my fingers ache.
Did I remember to lock the door?

The bus is late.

I wonder if I'll see her ever again.
If I send her another email, will she answer?
Probably not.

I'm not sure I locked the door and left food for Muffin.
She'll survive.

The lady with a cane got up when I sat on the bench.
Do I look creepy?
Did I zip up?
Just checked, I'm OK (now).

She still doesn't sit—
maybe, out of respect for an elder.

Like in Korea when that old lady made me take her seat.
Grabbed me and forced me down.
An old amazon, she was surprisingly strong.

I was grateful and amused.

Something is wrong with the bus stop!

A bulldozer left a pile of earth,
just ruined that little lawn.
Even under two feet of snow.

In two months, spring will come.
Maybe they'll fix it then.

Car in the River

Do I carry this stuff in my mind all the time?
God! it's my own personal Polonium,
just zapping away my DNA.
Mutating that perfect boy
into a little monster.

I guess that's why my "house" is crowded.

Snow on the backs of horses
the quiet of monster flakes

falling

falling

backed by black trees.

I focus on the road,
gripping the wheel,
blinded by whiteouts.

Didn't the road turn here?

I know this place.
I can see that car in the river.

It was here.

The car neatly parked.
The roof just above the ice,

but not enough.

Hunting in the Trailer Park

We were in Cascadia, Oregon that August, ours the smallest
trailer in the park. 110 in the shade, Canadians dying in the
heat, hoping for a breeze. Catty-corner to us, a neighbor in
a big Land Cruiser, so neat and tidy. His rig had a skirt, ugly
wheels hidden, a picket fence around a lawn, the only green
in the park. Next day it was 90, bringing such relief, happy for
the first time in days. And that morning he emerged, recently
showered, so well-groomed it could have been the '50s.

I watched him and wondered why he never looked at me. I
was prepared to wave till I understood.

I was invisible, ideal for a specialist of wildlife.

He was a hunter, crouching low, so intense, his steel glinting
in the morning sun, on the verge of primal action, killing for
noble purpose. He did not disappoint, wielding his perfect
scissors on that already-perfect grass.

Big White Dick.

Bouncing, ball, delight, rhythm, squeeze, squeeze, baleen,
    sperm, the white horror haunts me, the whale seen off
    the bow,
chased by our frail boat,

eye glaring at harpoon, racing to deep darkness.
That eye! That eye!

feeling pity for the tiny compass.
feeling anger at our misplaced hubris,

willing to destroy his beauty,
our beauty.

a doomed pursuit
of satisfaction in killing something

different.

a white mountain of that giant breed of fishes,
with brains the size of barrels.

O to have their beautiful minds.
to sing with them!

Flaming Plankton on a Moonless Night

Stripped of pretense in the soup.

Next to Iwagami in the Onsen
sharing hot love
from that big red faucet,

telling stories of failed missions,
lost hopes of any chance of salvation.

Telling stories of exile
to empty Arctic outposts.

My brother commands me, *go to the sea,*
pointing to the round door in the laundry.

I run across the sand crescent,
barefoot and naked on that painful beach

straight into the Black Sea.
Feeling cold darkness, my plunging body explodes
in a cathedral of light.

Burned by the silent green fire!
I weep in the sea
he knew.

War Heroes

He was gazing upwards.

It could have been a scene in a cathedral.
But it wasn't.

I saw him in the foyer of the Veterans Hospital.

He could have been Saint Augustine.
But he wasn't.

He was a veteran,
staring,
staring,
at nothing.

My dad was in a wheelchair.

In the picture I took,
he was sniffing
a magnolia blossom.

It was a couple of years before he died.

He said he would dream of the war.
(One minute someone would
be alive,

and suddenly ...)

He said he didn't make friends,

because he didn't want to get too close.

Also, he was their sergeant.

He took a shell fragment in his neck near the German border.

He recovered, more or less ...

mainly less.

Every other weekend the family would visit this hospital.

Marg and I would play chase on the lawn,

spy on the huge grey ships in Hampton roads.

Sometimes we would hand out lifesavers to the men.

The cigarettes were for the grown-ups.

Sometimes we would go to the show.

The men in wheelchairs lined the back of the auditorium.

Mom died before my dad.

When she found out she might be put in a wheelchair,

she ripped the tubes out of her arm.

Submarine

<an image>

Ghost riders cross a purple moon.

<dreamer>

His brow beads sweat,

it is the day of his death.

A nuclear monster thrums in his head.

He knows it's there, but he cannot hear it.

<fever dream>

32 angels of death

await release from a dark sea.

32 angels carry hell fires.

Fires of everlasting pain.

Fires that do not make way for new life.

Fires that mock Thanatos.

They are the death of many wives.

They are the scourge of innocent nations.

They are redeemers who bring nothing to the table.

Angel's wings of fire

Angel's wings of dead desire

Retribution.
Pointless death-upon-death
for the unlucky.
Shadow-lives for those who survive.

The angels smile.
Fire spills out of their mouths.

Begone, you bringers of life.
We are your fiery masters.

We command you to surrender
to our purpose.

We purge your planet of life and pain.
We leave pure crystals in our wake.

<lt>

The submarine, killer of nuclear monsters,
prowling deep depths at the mouth of the St. Lawrence.

A fox, silent, listening for the slightest sound.

Alert for nuclear whales,
destroyers of nations.

With kin sufficient
to destroy worlds—

something to bury in a well
and pretend an illusion.

Oh, the dark game we ignore.

It is too much to bear.

Custer's Last Stand!

Perhaps they will win.
We will succumb and learn from them.
We are the soft ones, and they know that.

They feel and we deal.
They cry and we die!
We are weak sisters—they are strong.

We want their love and they just want to be!
Strong enough to spit out babies big as watermelons
while we cower in some waiting room,

telling stories to the other frightened fellows
about things we shot.
But we are poets, *girly guys,* I guess.

Another mask to wear. Like a night in Venice.
Be someone else! That's the ticket!
The dog snorts. She's an "it." Got her priorities.

More focused than her "dad."
I can feel you cringing from 3,000 miles away.
Will you see this?

Probably.
You know boys need approval from their moms.
Cringed you again, didn't I!

Ha!

Yours truly,

B

Looking forward to tomorrow.

Who Am I This Morning?

Who I am, I do not know.
I float like a flake of snow.

Symmetry finds safer ground.
Home at last, but never found.

DTG 7305 (Days to Go)

I am writing with my new *Artist Loft 0.7 mm pen*. I wonder what we will say, today. Four elegant parts: 1-body, 2-refill, 3-spring and 4-removable tip. She is a beauty! No friction but the texture of the page. I am awestruck by her simplicity. She would be a goddess in the Kalahari. The gods were not crazy when they made her. A tube with a rubber grip. Inside, 4-mm wide ink in a transparent pipe with some mysterious clear goo topping the black, black stuff.

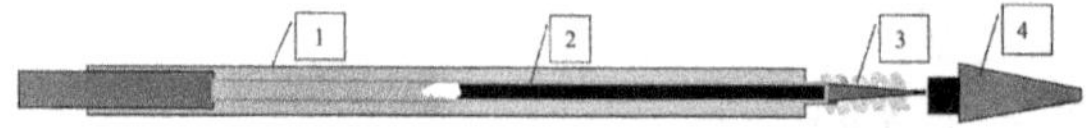

Can one be in love with a pen and not go to jail?

This morning I must pray to an imaginary Buddha. He lives in the folds of my brain-porridge, or in the legs of my old corpse. O my lord! I need your wisdom. What am I doing? Will I find the love I need so desperately? Will I find my mother? My dead mother who never seemed to want me. Who I could never be the right boy for.

Again, that f'in Rabbit Hole!

I am definitely in a rut. The dishwasher is disassembled in the kitchen. I don't know what to do. I will call the serviceman. It will cost me, but my own time costs me. I should start counting my days. I have a lot to do before I die.

I Am Not a Man

I cannot relate to sports on tv.
I hate the big fucking trucks.
I think he's an asshole thru and thru.

I hang with the women in the kitchen.
I smell people,
and flowers.

Yep, I'm not that guy,

and I'm proud of it.

My dad was a vet,
given to beating me.
He had this lucky charm,
a silver hand on a dick.

We found it in the box of old watches,
after the funeral.

That night, after a few drinks,
I threw it in the Chesapeake Bay.

Did I really do that?

Did he?

Somehow, the answer is always in me.
I smell it every day,
I run from it every minute.

Alone

With shattered memories
of horror and grace

I walk through the ashes of
burned-out ruins

and when
I can't stand it
any longer

the blue sky
takes me back.

Odysseus Fell Over

It had to do with the terrain of the moon.
Our eight-legged rocket tripped on a hole,
fell over, landed on a rock.

Lay there, whispering *I'm here, I'm here.*
Intuition could not prevent
this awkward predicament:

face down on lunar soil.

The sun is boiling my one side
my shadow side is freezing.

Night is coming, they
have no plans to save me.

Oh

I am fallen, unable to right myself.

Birthday Manifesto

I was in love once—
before I left the innocent forest
of my childhood.

Today my heart is empty.
Surrendered long ago.

Today I will wrestle my ghosts,

pin them to the mat,
whisper to them,

I love you.

Today I will burn a hole in my darkness,
with a fire of words.

For The Boys

In some film we were called Maggots
by the drill sergeant,
and we shouted:
"Yes Sir, Sergeant Sir!"

Was your dad a sergeant?
Was he like Robert's dad?

You know, Robert—
who was hustled off to the psyche ward in '68,
for dropping books on the floor of Mincers,
trying to prove he could be spontaneous.

That day, a page in my journal
was smeared with blood from a papercut.
I don't know what this has to do with anything,
or even if I was there.

I can see the flashing lights,
as if I had been a spectator at the back of the crowd.
I watched them strap him to the stretcher,
too frozen to run in and help.

When I told the shrink about Bob's struggle to be
    spontaneous,
he didn't seem to care.

He said Bob's past was irrelevant,

but I remember
his dad's laughter as he taunted:

"Take a swing,"

and remember Bob's skinny arms flailing so pathetically,
trying and trying,
and his dad
egging him on,
that big marine hand
clamped on his head.

Later I heard that when his brother committed suicide
it was blamed on drugs.
And for some strange reason,
I remember that when Mike was five,

his aunt seduced him.

And he told me he liked
the way she rubbed his dick.
And that for a while I was jealous.

For a while

until the memories came.

Kitsune Tea

Suzuki said: if you try hard enough you will remember the future.

1. Dreamtime

Early morning, I am eating numbers.

Kitsune smiles, I fractalize spinach.

Fancy that,
clocks on a clothesline
droopy pancakes on a wire
warping time and space
in one place

The Physicist pulls on his beard
and has another
glass of
wine

It's all going to stop someday,
it all has to stop!

Even the noise on

2. Kitsune

In the trees, sipping tea, she came to me, telling tales so old, like the feathers in that coat she wore, interwoven with obsidian beads peering like raven eyes.

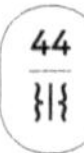

It was a tale of madness.

This remembering brings shudders,

yet it also brings delight.

It all must stop, said Kitsune. *It must stop or I'll go mad.* I think she got that wrong—she is already mad. I can see it in the red in her eyes, those drops of saliva on her chin. She is looney as a kite. Flying in circles, ragged tails following her, wicked circling, twirling madly in the shuddering wind.

Mad, mad, my dear friend is mad.

And, I love her madness.

But I'm not mad, am I? I feel perfectly sane. I put one shoe on at a time. Sandals really, but no matter. I'm not mad.

Not even a little bit.

I wonder what oysters think. Clinging as they do to the barnacled jetties. Pounded by the ocean mother who talks to us with her thudding thighs. Her rolling body crunching down and down.

    Salt sprays in my eyes
      I pray I'm not mad—

like the rabbit with the grey hat, who defines madness with his wacky chatter. Never shutting up. Hopping around like water on a skillet. He's a crazy one. Not like me. I'm serious. Counting my toes and fingers. Neat and tidy. All there.

So? Suzuki counters. *Who really gives a damn what you surmise? You have sand in your eyes. You all do. You're right about one thing, though. It all has to end.*

Otherwise we cannot begin.

3. Emergence

At first it was invisible except to a dreamer. To others, every-
    thing looked dead.
The trees, dead. The earth did not sigh. The sky was not
    there. The sun hid his face.

Dead, Dead, Dead.

Except in the fool's head.

That morning, he saw it on the branch—
little fuzzy balls cupped in green tea leaves.
So innocuous he hardly noticed.

Something different in the screen of trees.

A softness—
    that seemed like nothing.

Can you not imagine the thunder of a million tiny things
    growing?

Reaching for the grey dawn.

The light,

oh,

the painful light

    reaching
        reaching
            reaching

4. Spring

A shot of whiskey at breakfast. He feels it in his nose.
Screaming at the reappeared sky. Winter's gone, except for
pockets of snow in deep shadows.

Rain keeps him at bay, but he goes out anyway. It is back!

Water flows in the dead fields. The trees seem like smoke.
Pink plumes appear in the hazy forest. Volcanic eruptions
speak of something coming.

He sees a raven in his neighbor's tree. Those obsidian eyes

tell him to rise. *Fight the day. You must live.*

He feels Kitsune now. Her madness is gone. She has purpose
    now.
It swells in her. The world carries her.
Their mother speaks in tongues. Her divine madness pos-
    sesses the land. Passion seizes us. We walk together
    toward the sun.

5, Summer

What happened? It was spring yesterday!

The rains came. Green monsters shadow the forest.
I am possessed by flowers. They can wait no longer.

Her kits are yipping. A rabbit twitches one last time in her
    jaws.
No remorse is seen. A circle completed.

My sadness consumes me. I fear my remembered future.

A trout flies frozen in midair above the dam. It is pulled by
    invisible strings towards the divine imperative.

Multiply and die.

Spinning intensity rocks the land.

The earth groans and splits. Mountains rise,

reaching.

6. Fall

Over so soon!
Not really.
We are not in a hurry.

To celebrate
as we fade,
put on a show of resistance,

to not go gently.

We light firecrackers and bonfires.

Sing to the stars.

Treasure these lost days,
celebrate something sacred
something dying,
but not gone.

Why are the last days coloured when we
should be fearing the inevitable?

It is not a time to worry.

We abandon ourselves to those bright days.

Impermanence sharpens our senses.
We savor our last meals.

We diminish,
but are glorious.

7. Winter

The far shore beckons.

A heart yearns for silence.

Winter's gusts rattle the window where the raven sat.

Kitsune whispers, *come visit us, we are waiting.*

Breathing green fire,
    foxes play at midnight.

Autumn

plasmas of charged particles,
swarming spots of black birds
coalesce into
fingers of grey matter.

Translucent snakes twist and turn,
backlit by fading sky.
A vision held safely

in the bosom of approaching night.

Love Children of Space & Time

I am the son of space,
you are the daughter of time.

Together we dance around stars,
boogie by black holes—

cure inflexible light beams.

We are the dynamic duo,
we can defeat linear gravity.

We bend the heavens to our dance.

We define your reality
with relativity.

We bring the blackness of blackness,
a beautiful nothingness,
to the centre of galaxies.

We rule by our game of hide and seek.

We work together to make peace
where love is universal,
time stretches
gravity warps
space-time,
things
are

&
light
emerges
triumphant.

Traveling to the Start-Up Fair

4 PM. It is safe to drive. Snow's piled up but plows have
    finished.
Saaif makes way in the rented Tesla, autopilot off.

Dusk shines in the city.

It seems a year since we started this trip to the start-up fair.
Dressed to kill, not knowing an enemy, but ready to hunt.

Night falls in the city.

Seeking money, recognition, and something undefined,
    prosperity,
companionship, deliverance of loneliness, even true love.

Lights abound in the city.

Our destination promises all things, and more … *blue sky* say
    the VCs.
Strawberry fields say the marketers, *forever and a day*.

Sex everywhere in the city.

As we near our destination my mind asks me, *what were you
    thinking?*
My heart answers. *Nothing at all.*

Emptiness abounds in the city.

My imagined goddess, sitting, elbow on one knee, eyes half
shut, smiling.
On a city side street, lights reflect off her frozen lamppost.

A white raven prays.

The Wise One Is Here

A clack of sticks to focus elsewhere, to take me to nothing-
ness. It is not important. It is just there. It cannot touch you.
It is in your imagination. It is all in your imagination. You want
it to be real so you will not be crazy, but it is not real now.

It is imagination and memory—that's the nature of the beast,
your beast. Imagination and memory. You reconstruct a
probable past from each. A combination.

It is the way the processor works.

Do not fight it.

Surf the wave.

This Morning,

it is February third.
Buckle up—
don't escape on me, now!

I think I have something to say,
but don't know what it is yet.

I just finished listening to Plath, Bukowski, Thomas—
that lot of self-involved assholes.
Makes me want to puke,
want to write stuff that sticks to
your shoes.
Feeling dizzy,

fear of exposure ...

Trees fall! FUCK!
Think I'll stop

and save you
the trouble.
But I can't

for some reason.
What is going on (wrong) with me?

They are all writing about death

and I want to put my mind

in a machine.

Some want death,

want to surrender to its allure.

Clueless.

Think I'll take that nap now.

Only got 4 hours of sleep last night ... yeah. Bye.
I will take a nap, wake up
and eat some pie.

Japan

Photos, Japan, reminiscent of vaginas, wet, folded,
disturbed symmetry, fungible, sea smell, wrinkled tunnels,
return, taste, touch, eat, drink, nibble, pile of pears,
octopus swirl, strong, clinching, called pussy, but really
the hand of the goddess. Steals life, grasps continuity,
    speaker
in tongues. Now to sleep.
}|{

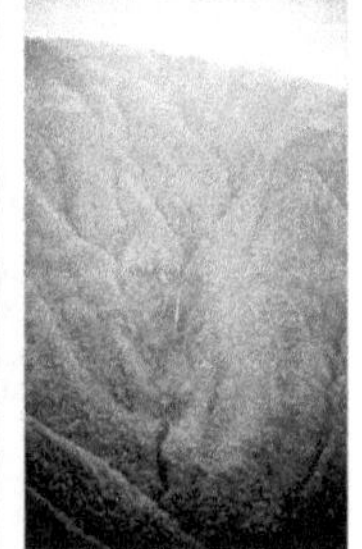

Photos by Bill Morrow.
Top left:Sakurajima Volcano
near Kagoshima, Japan, 1992.
Top right: View from Summit
of Galeras Volcano (near Pasto,
Colombia, 1993, 3 days before
eruption). Left: Tree roots
embracing (Barrie, Ontario,
2023)

Conversations with CC 1

my dick and I chat about pussies,

how they are so much like flowers

their aromatic folds seeking communion,

tickled pink by our attention.

together, we are transfixed by them,
like dogs staring at bacon.

he tells me he misses them.
he tells me he's scared
of how much he wants to swim
in their salty waves.

I treasure his directness.
I treasure his inappropriateness.
he is my little puppy.
ready to bite monsters.

beautiful women have said to me,
I don't understand what men are thinking.

I struggle to think of a true answer.
my mind's eye

keeps staring at bacon.

Those Cardinal Virtues

Faith

I know I'm going to die, and I have doubts
about an extension to another dimension.

So, this faith thing has a low bar.

I don't have a thing for mysteries except
for ones that come
from damaged nervous systems.

But I do believe, in a qualified goodness

I find mainly in dogs.

Jury's out on the rest.

Hope

Truly, I can't give up my search for
the perfect stranger who just validates
what I am.

I don't expect her to feel my pain.
I just need her to confirm I'm not a freak.

And also a bit of love
would be appreciated.

I've graduated from

the unconscious phase,
more or less,
but I'm
still following

trails of obsession.

But reining them in
as best I can.

Charity

I'm trying.

I dutifully
give my wife
a check.

Know it doesn't count.

I adopted orphans.
It was my first's idea,
just went along but enjoyed it.

So kinda a selfish thing.
But the kids like me
so maybe counts a little.

I'm
a tree hugger
but still use gas,

and I'm gonna fly to Europe

to clean up the Baltic,

and drink good beer.

So lately I've been nice

to strangers

but with a motive

of running into one.

Re Hope ... see above

They Canceled Pluto

Not a planet! they said.

Too eccentric! they said.

Travels to strange places! they said.

Out of the plane of the rest!

(Out of the elliptic—
a poorly stacked plate in their china cabinet.)

And too small! they said.

Smaller than our moon!

Pluto is special, I say.

A place of methane glaciers,

a place of crystal mountains

and flash-frozen seas of air.

Holding, perhaps, a vast ocean of good ol'
H2O under the snow.

WOW! I say,

Gotta get on that Pluto bus!

 Are you with me, Fellow Plutonians!

(Loki, Loki-motioning. Can't help hizself.)

Full Moon Beach

In the windswept night
the blackened sea burns his eyes.

bobbing small, far offshore,
a tiny cell in an infinite plasma.

seeing his wave he strokes wildly
to find her rolling trough.

thrusting water backwards
circling arms, kicking

to find that place where the sea
slides down her slope,

and suddenly.
he's flying
arms extended

hands like skis

skimming through foam.
riding the crashing light

till the sea spits him
from her turbulent womb.

banishing him on the silver beach.

reborn, spitting out brine.

Not a Happy Me

Woe is me said the sailor who has sailed hearts across the

barren ocean.

Oh, Oh, Oh, where does this stream go?

Oh my, I'm going to die and go to that lost continent

we've all heard of, but do not know much about,

a place of grace or doom

a place of solitude and separation from

the sprawling splendor

of this place we call love.

Notes from the Sled to Oblivion

I am speeding up,
wasn't expecting that,
faster down the slope.
What if I hit something!
What if I don't!

I may be going so fast,
kill myself in a mighty crash.
If I don't slow down
somehow, I'll break through
some sound barrier and
go somewhere (alone, home, above).

I just woke up. My eyes are
swirly, that arc of ripples.
Don't want to know what it is.

Remember, Francis had a brain tumour,
Benign, not like Louis'—
his killed him in a few weeks. Better not to know.

If it's incurable, better to deny deny.
What if it can be fixed?
What then? Maybe it's better to know.
Get some time to get ready.

Bukowski wrote that thing about dying,
really gripping but kind of crappy,

the truest stuff is garbage.

Whimpering on the way.
Brain on fire, those ripples persist.
    I know they'll go away, so
        I can ignore them like before.

Shit! What if they don't go away,
        then I'll be a fine mess!
        Muff raises her head.
                Might as well get up.

Go for a walk,
        forget about it, or would,
        except I wrote it down!
                Fuck!

I wrote it down, so it will stare at me!
        Idiot! Can't do denial properly!
        Jeeze! That crazy poet played
                it like a game, Fucking

Romantic, to love the idea of croaking.
        Idiots! It's not a game, like
        that monk said, *there is no rehearsal.*
The real deal only ends one way—
        under your Jesus!

It's gone now. Should I talk to Nelson? (I did talk to Nelson.)

(Next day, waking up, wrote this)

Her face stays with me,
music in the distance
across a field.

Mozart playing,
I went to her and sat.

She looked at me and understood.

She touched the beauty with me.
We sat together.

I knew her and she knew me,
inhabitants of the Border Land,
watching those slaves of belief
in terrible things,
torches blazing, arms in salute,

Don't they know?

The music floats above us
caressing our bodies
speaking to us

Oh Marcia, you are here!
I am so sorry I did not hold you.
It is too late now.
Forgive me, oh sweet one.

Judith's daughter held me,
we walked together.

genesis

The light shines between her legs
and he is starstruck, given breath
by Pillars of Creation.

Imagining his hand
gazing,
brushing her mystery.

Gobsmacked by ultraviolet days
relentlessly unfolding,
glory from the death of atoms.

Lyman-alpha finds icy moons
and back alleys of comets
tickling atoms.

Atoms complex in random ways,
tiny gods rolling dice,
sepia stains, Sagan's daughters,

Tholins, born of feckless molecules.

The comet faces her hot star.
Wings blowing backward
comet babies ... moon children
fall to the blue ball.

Carbon blooms, aeons pass,
a green shadow
erupts in the sea.

(aeons pass)

Artery's pulsing, the lonely traveler
pumps iron of a different kind.
A liquid kind—Hema.

An artist watches mist assemble
thunder and light in mountains.
An imagined spark flies
from the finger of a reaching giant.

Now so quiet, thunder forgotten,
the saved us is rescued
from eternal entropy.

A writer's ears sing like seagulls
creaking over turbulent waters.
alive above fevered oceans

Outer space beckons,
calls him home;
calls him
to the place he started.

〕l〔

Movable Feast

The thing
about science

is that you
can eat it.

Like a juicy
chunk of meat
or *crème fraîche*
and strawberries.

So delish,
such satisfaction
and so necessary—

It's the real deal!

Not like poetry

which really
keeps you lost,

being so fucking real
in spite of itself.

My present to you is this secret.

Most people think E=mc² was the big discovery.

(physicists have a little
secret.)

The big one, the real deal,
is this one, the Einstein Field Equation:

(how) the SHAPE of the Space-Time continuum
creates the FORCES of Gravity and Motion—
explains the bending of light around stars // black holes.

$$R_{\mu\nu} - \frac{1}{2} R\, g_{\mu\nu} = \frac{8\pi G\, T_{\mu\nu}}{c^2}$$

(pretty much defining the universe.)

This equation swept away Newton in a magnificent Tsunami
    of time and space.

The shape of Space-Time
creating forces, daunting us
bending us, invisibly,
weighing our homes,
caressing our sight
holding us, weakly,
whispering
prayers, quiet.

Haiku

Mourning Dove Down

grounded in the street

gently, I put her on a branch

the look she gave me

Later That Week

flapping and cooing

the dove took off, that afternoon

my struggle began

Dove Again

same place in the street

she flaps her wings and rises

leaving notes behind

Winter is Coming

stillness surrounds me

tree shadows touching neighbors

I feel such longing

Homeless at VA Beach 1967

under the fishing pier

I try to sleep in the sand

and hope I'm alone

1992

Highway to Mexico
tossing empties out the window
can't outrun myself

The Memory

it was the same place in the street
where I found the first dove

she flapped her wings
and pulsed into the sky

with that cooing sound
I struggle to describe

in my mind, afterwards,
it became so quiet, yet

Threshold of Discovery

I move my feet under the bed cover and

she stares like Einstein on the threshold of discovery.

Judyth, I forgot to tell you I saw a raven,

a big motherfucker, right downtown,
through my windshield,
arcing upwards, eruption of black wings
flapping, fingers reaching,

arcing imperious, beak slightly curved,
stone eye relentless,
dancing right in front of me.

A giant message—meaning what?

Or an arctic crow lost, on his way somewhere.

Don't Forget

Happiness floats by like coloured leaves in that river as you drown ... don't forget to enjoy them as you go under.

Tanka

Perfection Lost

On the June evening,
a butterfly flexes perfect wings.
Whoosh goes my net!

As I pin it to my cold wall,
iridescence stains my fingers.

Little People (two Tanka)

Toy house on a stump,
backyard woodshop in August,
pine trees whispering.

Leprechauns must be sleeping,
dreaming of gold and mischief.

I am thinking of
putting a pot of the good stuff
out front, this dark night.

It seems like the least I could do
to ward off some wee havoc.

Their Fearless Leader

Safely ensconced

in his Florida mansion

the croc weeps again.

Endangered, as usual, in

the same old boring movie.

}|{

mom & dad

Red hair, smell of whiskey

"Henry do something about that child!"

The lawnmower cord, knotted at one end.

No place to go.

)|(

Two Empaths,

like those neutron stars
spiral together

until they consume one another.

Their mutual gravity
bending space
till no light can escape

except a steady drip
of Schrödinger's
madness—

the kat
smiles broadly
in the box

no one
cares.

Sandy Hook 10th Anniversary

My children,
where are you?

It's been years.
Where are you?

What could I have done?

I stare at a door
that never opens.

Every Breath

You may think I am immersed in self-pity.
I am not.

Every breath is precious.
Every remembrance,
even the horror,
is testimony to my survival,
my consciousness,
my loving.

But my door is broken,
and the universe comes in,
washing me in the sea of living things.

Alive in countless thoughts,
I swim through life,

see beauty everywhere.

The wound in me persists.

But I am still alive.
Still here.

Floating in a sea of
Nothing

and Something.

Aware of this beautiful contradiction

some call love.

Alone in this cathedral.

My friends,

you must surrender

to this beautiful illusion.

You must imagine the soaring columns.
Smell the incense
let the soulful
chanting
carry you.

Dear Reader

… ho, hoe, toe, together, GRATITUDE, platitude, story, hoary, Christmas, scrooge, sponge, tongue, taste, baste, paste, practice, distract, abstract,

Taste the flowers of the world.
Smell the armpits of the planet.
Measure nothing; calculate it!
Put nothing in a box.

Quantify nothingness.
Smell the glorious nothingness of existence!
Tramp on the glorious grass.
Pee on the lawn!

Turn the page on life.
Find something new, something that breaks *the ordinary*.
A vision of the future, a vision of simple beauty, of singular
    taste.

A cathedral of light

My inner home where I pray and play my desperate game.

Oh I love you. Oh I need you dear reader!
I need you to witness my hapless joy, my tears and fears.
I need you to know me. I need you to learn my ways.

I need you to exist when I am no longer here.

I need your murmur and ire. I need your poison and hate.

I need your yin yang and game.

I am watching over you. I am walking under you.

I am the ghost with the most!

I am the idiot who stumbles down the alley.
I am the jumble of flesh who begs on the highway.

I am the man who holds the homeless sign.

I am lost and need you to find me!

What Nothing!

House of Forgotten Dreams

Guanyin, Goddess of compassion, help me!
I am something, a piece of some star that had
the impertinence to think. Broken. I feel awe at
the majesty of my ether. Strive to be whole. To have
gravity. I am a planet with a moon who comforts
me. My moon speaks to me of the lonely heavens. She
tells me she loves me—I yearn for her, always.
Seek her love, live for her silent laughter.
Feel her tears as she mourns for our sorry species.
Feel her continuously breathing joy.
Shadow lover talking to me in my dreams.

Stopping now,
nothing is here.
The quiet
raven
waits
patiently.

I hear his crow cousins slice silence with their caws,
echoing cries of others in the cloudy dusk.
Their sounds stay with me. I see them hurry off with
secret purpose. I feel kinship. Feel love in that emptiness
as they fly away on some mission. Maybe they
delight in some dead thing. Some squirrel who met a sudden
end on the highway. They are night watchmen who
tidy up after us. Clean up the death we bring.
Those ignored lives we disdain.

My meandering brain will not shut up. I want to be free
of its relentless chatter. That background noise about
a million important things. Talk I cannot cope with.
A rabbit hole of obsession where I forget
myself, lost to a shiny object or tasty treat. Some
bobble. Lost to my own presence. Lost to
some memory of

      No wonder I yearn for nothing.
        The silence of the grave
          does not scare me.
            I yearn for it.
              I learned to do that
                when

I am defined by my forgotten dreams.
Buried in my porridge. That grey slop between my ears.

<sketch of weeping man>

You may think I am immersed in self-pity. I am not.
Every breath is beautiful.
Every remembrance, wonderful.
Even the horror
is testimony
to survival
consciousness
continuity
love.

My door is broken and the universe comes in. I
am awash in a sea of living things. Alive
in my countless thoughts. I swim through life.
Feel currents around me. See beauty everywhere.
 The wound in me persists.
 The damage stays.
 But I am still alive.
 I am here,
 alive in a sea
 nothing
 and
 something.
Aware of this beautiful contradiction.

Alone in this cathedral.

Thanks for Nothing

She sleeps in atoms and galaxies,
    between electrons and stars.
Sweet emptiness,
    by-product of weak gravity
found in quantum furrows,
    empty space for cosmic poets.

Mocking, Einstein called her *Gespensterfelder*—
Ghost Waves haunting shadows,
making her defenseless,
    by definition, doomed, but not dead,
she laughs at the ridiculousness of Multiverse,
    who neither speaks nor listens.

Acknowledgments

Thank you to Judyth Hill, my guide, mentor, and friend; my deep, dear friend Kelly Watt who set me on this journey; and Mary Meade and Wild Rising Press who brought it all together...

Gratitude to the members of our Taos poetry group, including Rebekah Ventura, Randy Dills, Zoë Bird, Brenda Wildrick, Tarn Granucci, Lynne Ford, and Madhuri Martin; my dear children Kim and Holly, my sister Marg, my lost-now-found friend Meg, my Canadian friends Norm, Peg, and John, my breakfast club; Richard and Eleanor who inspired me, Mike who gets me, my nephew Ken who gets it, and my cousin Theanne who understands where it comes from.

And finally, my friend Lauren, who kept me alive.

Author's Biography

Bill Morrow has spent a lifetime seeking light. He is an Applied Physicist whose seminal thesis on "Correlation Spectroscopy" developed mathematical tools and instrumentation to use light to measure atmospheric gases. Over more than 50 years, he has created new tools to measure atmospheric constituents from orbit, assist measuring Relativistic warping of space, characterize the spectra of Femtosecond lasers, deactivate airborne virus, and simulate the synthesis of organic materials on the Jovian Moon, Europa.

Now, in his twilight, his poetry reaches for the light between atoms, stars, moons, and us.

While he has written poetry since his youth, this is his first formal publication in the genre.

The body text is set in Iskra Light, designed by Tom Grace of TypeTogether. Luminous, lively, buoyant, with clean, bright edges: apt descriptions for this font and the poetry in Bill Morrow's debut collection, *Kitsune Tea.*

Iskra is a sans serif typeface that teases the border between unadorned and ornamental; the word "Iskra" in Russian translates as "the vital spark" or "flash" signifying the inner spiritual spark that ignites change, again, an exquisite resonance with Morrow's work which leaps, in quantum surprise, from uniquely original thought to image and onward, with, so often, a glint, a glamour, a gleam of humor. Described as "possessing a distinct flair" and "a study of bridled energy," Iskra's forms pay warm, subtle homage to brush lettering, echoing the graceful curves, balanced proportions, and playful asymmetry present in work from an artist's hand—just as this collection is lit by Morrow's own revelatory pen and ink drawings.

The titles in Kitsune Tea are set in Mukta Mahee, designed by Shuchita Grover and Noopur Datye of Ek Type, a collaborative type design studio based in Mumbai. Mukta is a contemporary, "humanist," "mono-linear" (meaning strokes of consistent thickness) typeface family, created to support Devanagari, Gujarati, Gurumukhi, Tamil, and Latin scripts; a font also inspired by and emulating the look of handwritten letters, mimicking the angles at which a right-handed person holds a pen, giving it an organic, calligraphy-like appearance. This font was created to grant expressive possibilities in the major languages of India, echoing an underpinning that threads through these poems...the wondrous unity available to a poet through a rich multiplicity of vision.